Sound Locators, Fire Control Systems and Searchlights of the Heavy Flak

150 cm searchlights during a spotting exercise.

Werner Müller

Schiffer Military/Aviation History
Atglen, PA

Sources

Koch, Horst-Adalbert "Flak" Podzun-Pallas-Verlag, Friedberg, 2nd ed. 1965
Kuhlenkamp, Alfred "Flak-Kommandogeräte" VDI-Verlag, Berlin 1943
Muther, Alfred "Das Gerät der leichten Artillerie vor, in und nach dem Weltkrieg" Part IV of Flugabwehrwaffen, Bernard und Graefe Verlag, Berlin 1929
Nicolaisen, Dr. Hans-Dietrich "Der Einsatz der Luftwaffen- und Marinehelfer im 2. Weltkrieg" published privately, Büsum 1981
Pickert, Wolfgang "Unsere Flakartillerie", Mittler Verlag, Berlin 1940
Renz, Otto Wilhelm v. "Deutsche Flugabwehr im 20. Jahrhundert", Mittler Verlag, Frankfurt 1960
Kriegsgeschichtliche Einzelschriften der Luftwaffe, "Die Entwicklung und Einsatz der deutschen Flakwaffe und des Luftschutzes im Weltkrieg" Vol. 1, Mittler Verlag, Berlin 1938
Mitteilungen für Freunde und Förderer des Museums für historische Wehrtechnik e.V., Nuremberg, Nos. 20 through 27
Luftwaffe service manuals (Luftwaffendienstvorschriften, abbr. L.Dv.)
L.Dv.400/4a, L.Dv.400/4b, L.Dv.400/5b, L.Dv.601/1, L.Dv.602/1, L.Dv.602/2, L.Dv.607, L.Dv.615, L.Dv.T.1252/2, L.Dv.T.1300, L.Dv.T.1303, L.Dv.T.1350/1, L.Dv.T.1350/2, L.Dv.T.1351, L.Dv.T1352/1, L.Dv.T.1352/2

Photo Credits

Archives of the Museum für historische Wehrtechnik, Nuremberg (photos by Karl Werner)
Bundesarchiv Koblenz
Bundesarchiv-Militärarchiv Freiburg
Muther, Alfred "Das Gerät der leichten Artillerie vor, in und nach dem Weltkrieg" Part IV of Flugabwehr, supplement, Bernard und Graefe Verlag, Berlin 1929
Wehrtechnische Studiensammlung Koblenz
Central Archives of Jenaoptik Carl Zeiss GmbH Jena
VDI special edition "Flugabwehr"
From the private archives of: Fleischer, Wolfgang; Hümmelchen, Dr. Gerhard; Otte, Alfred; Rösch, Helmut and Suhany, Volker
Luftwaffe service manuals and the "Vorläufige Beschreibung des Kommandogerätes 40", parts 1, 2 and 3, Berlin 1940

For their valuable contributions the author wishes to thank: Dr. Werner Blatter, Alzey; Wilhelm Kleinen, Illertissen; Prof. Dr. Wolfgang Sawodny, Elchingen; Dipl.-Ing. Werner Sünkel, Leinburg; Elmar Widmann, Apfeltrach.

A Kommandogerät 40 with radar.

Translated from the German by Don Cox

Printed in China.
ISBN: 0-7643-0568-9

This book was originally published under the title,
Waffen Arsenal-Horchgeräte-Kommandogeräte und Scheinwerfer der schweren Flak
by Podzun-Pallas Verlag.

We are interested in hearing from authors with book ideas on related topics.

Published by Schiffer Publishing Ltd.
4880 Lower Valley Road
Atglen, PA 19310
Phone: (610) 593-1777
FAX: (610) 593-2002
E-mail: Schifferbk@aol.com
Please write for a free catalog.
This book may be purchased from the publisher.
Please include $3.95 postage.
Try your bookstore first.

AAA Targeting Systems During the First World War

When engaging a target moving in a free space, not only does azimuth and range have to be considered (as with ground artillery), but elevation must also be factored in as a third dimension. The precise location of the target can only be determined by measuring the azimuth from a base direction (usually due north), or by measuring the elevation above the horizon in conjunction with the range. In order to hit the target, estimations have to be fed to the gun for the point in space which would be occupied by the target at the end of the artillery shell's flight time. Assuming, of course, that the intended victim does not alter its course, speed, or elevation from the time the shell is fired until it detonates.

During the First World War, these predictor values were passed to the gunner and his crew, who sighted the gun directly based on measured or estimated range. The values were a) elevation adjustment, b) correction setting(high or low), c) lateral deviation(right or left), and d) fuze burn time; values a and d were determined from range finding, while values b and c were estimates made from experience. Approach values for the guns could be taken from command tables, which were graduated in 500 meter increments for various target altitudes up to 2500 meters and included ranges in 1000 meter increments out to 5000 meters. The tables also showed target speeds of 10, 20 , 30 and 40 meters per second, plus had a space for entering the time of firing, setting of the gun and fuze setting (for burn time, used to determine the predictor values). These assigned values were for direct firing of the guns and were sighted using complicated adjusting mechanisms, which varied in design with virtually every gun type. In such a manner the line of sight to the target and the barrel's axis could be adjusted independent of each other.

However, increasing target speeds and altitudes made lead distances from the time the firing order was given until the round arrived in the target area too great. Determining the elevation angle was also becoming less accurate and front line troops began demanding a mechanism with which the predictor values could immediately be calculated and read.

In the autumn of 1915 the first such plotting device was introduced, the "Peres" lead plotter (named after its inventor). With it, the impact point could be determined with the prerequisite that the target maintained a horizontal, straight and uniform flight path.

The lead plotter consisted of a telescope with a graduated circle, or gauge, and base mount with a stopwatch and chart, on which was entered the distances corresponding to the shell flight time.

In 1916 this was followed by a command chart, from which the necessary burn time and elevation data could be instantly read. Nevertheless, despite these measures it was discovered that there were still far too many shortcomings with direct firing. No longer was it always possible for the gunner to sight and track his targets, which were becoming less and less easy to identify due to their higher operating altitudes and camouflage schemes.

Accordingly, in 1917 the "Jakob" command table was developed for indirect firing, whereby the gun was aimed at the anticipated impact point without the gunner having to see the target. Using this system the target was sighted directly with a telescope and the target point was determined by rangefinding at the point of intersection with the height arm. The height finder on the range finding apparatus provided the target's altitude. Impact point was calculated based on the lead of the target. Values for the gun elevation and fuze burn time settings were read off the viewboard and passed to the gun crews. In a policy implementation by the Commanding General of the Air Forces (Kogenluft) dated 30 October 1917 the device was made availabe on a wide-scale basis for all heavy AAA units.

Below: Adjusting controls for a 10.5 cm O.-Flak L/35 built by Rheinmetall during the First World War.

Below: The "Jakob" command board with scope, height arm and viewplate showing overall barrel elevation and fuze setting.

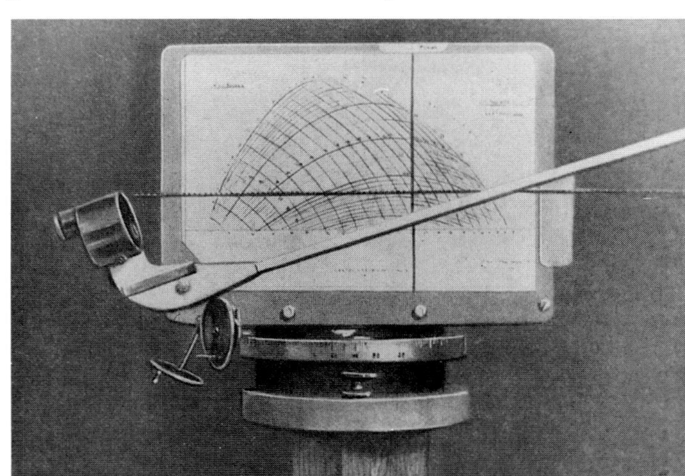

In 1916 Reserve Offizier Schönian developed a lead plotter which was named after him, similar to the "Peres" lead plotter and because of that never put into production. Schönian improved upon his device, making it into a command system for direct and indirect firing. It was built by Zeiss Jena and tested at the beginning of 1918. However, since Kogenluft had in the interim ordered that all command systems be designed exclusively for indirect sighting, Schönian's device was never put into series production. His subsequent newly-designed "Flak Kommando-Gerät Schönian 1919" did not make it to the front line troops for trials before the war's end.

It is also worth mentioning another system, that built by Pschorr, which was not put into series production but later formed the basis for the development of the Kommandogerät 36.

The significant difference between a device for direct firing and one for indirect firing is that with the former system the target is tracked with the aid of a sighting mechanism on the gun. In order to determine the point of impact it is not only necessary to calculate the burn length (later, following the introduction of time delay fuzes, the fuze running time), but also the lead factor has to be input to the automatic corrector along with lateral deviation, all done on a case by case basis. On the other hand, indirect firing incorporates a command device located separately from the gun, which passes and constantly updates all data required for the impact point to the guns (either by radio or using a data transmission system. This data includes collective gun elevation, impact azimuth and the fuze running time/burn time. This latter system means that the guns are not sighted individually and at the same time are ready for firing at a moment's notice.

Above: The Flak-Kommandogerät Schönian 1918 built by the company of Zeiss Jena. View is of the right side. Its performance figures were: target ranges from 2000 to 11000 meters, target altitudes from 1000 to 6000 meters, elevation angles between 10° and 70° and target speeds from around 0 to 50 meters per second. The greatest lead range was around 2000 meters.

Below: The Flak-Kommandogerät Schönian 1918 in position, being operated by its four-man crew.

Below: The Peres lead plotter, here the model Am 17, built by the Zeiss Jena firm and consisting of a scope with height finder and azimuth scale, an elevation dial and a base mount. Not shown is the associated stopwatch with chart, on which the shell flight times corresponding to the ranges were entered, and a command board, from which the burn time and elevation were read after compensating for the target height and correction count.

Hand in hand with the development of command systems for indirect firing were efforts to pass the control data to the guns without time delay or possible misunderstandings such as might occur over telephone or radio. Such transmission systems were called "central sighting mechanisms" and later "data transmission systems" during World War One. With the "Schnetzler" electric remote control system the guns were given the requisite elevation and azimuth adjustments automatically; the gun crews only needed to set the fuzes, load and fire.

Very soon, however, problems began cropping up with the heavy and cumbersome devices - necessary for adjusting the azimuth and elevation of the guns - and it wasn't long before crews began pining for more simplified transmission alternatives. The follow-the-pointer system used a low-voltage current to pass constantly updated data from the azimuth and elevation pointer positions on the command device to pointers. The guns' manually operated azimuth and elevation controls were linked to the follow-the-pointer gauges, which had to be brought into coincidence with each other by adjusting the gun controls. Here, too, the war's end brought a halt to the necessary testing, particularly since the Treaty of Versailles prohibited the Reichswehr from developing AAA weapons and command systems.

It should be pointed out that the development of command and so-called central sighting systems during the First World War only really got underway during the war's last few years. The reason for this was most likely that the importance of indirect sighting was only recognized at a relatively late stage. Although several systems were proposed before the end of the war, none of them ever reached truly operational status. The wish for a system which combined command, control and measuring functions into one (the later data transmission system) remained unfulfilled and it wasn't until much later that such a system was realized.

Range finders (Entfernungsmesser, or EM)

One of the prerequisites for engaging airborne targets was the accurate relay of precise range. During the first two years of the First World war this function was fulfilled by the inverted image range finder common to the field artillery (Em. Felda), having a horizontal base of 1.25 meters and 18x magnification. The system was mounted on a tripod and weighed 15 kg. Accurate ranging data was possible out to ao¶istance of 4000 meters.

As this device became less and less effective with the increasing target altitudes, from 1916 a two-meter inverted image range finder was introduced which provided useable data out to a slant range of 6,000 meters. Here, too, magnification was 18x and the device weighed around 16 kg.

Near the end of the war the Königliche Zugflak 88 mm and 105 mm units were supplied with an inverted image range finder with a 4 meter base and 20x magnification.

The inverted image range finder provides two picture fields, one right side up and the other upside down. The same points in both fields must be brought into alignment by rotating a calibration key device using a calibration knob along a dividing line. Thus the angle to the target, equal to the inverse value of the range, was determined. This was often quite difficult, if not impossible, to determine with a small, rapidly moving target, particularly so when the target was being observed with only one eye. Accordingly, then, the Flak's preferred system was the stereoscopic range finder used by the Kriegsmarine during the First World War. With these devices the calibration was determined by the ability to use both eyes to spot the object visually, whereby the eye separation is magnified onto the particular range finder's base length. Also, by moving a calibration wheel calibration marks can be brought into alignment with the target, in which two lines of sighting projecting from the base ends are laid over the target. Distance can then be measured from the resulting angle. A detailed description of the

Left: An improved variant of the "Peres" lead plotter of the First World War was used up until around 1936, first in a disguised form by the Reichswehr and then by the Flak.

Below: The viewfinder of an inverted image range finder. On the left is the view of the target before calibration, while on the right shows it following calibration. Drift = constant 1/e

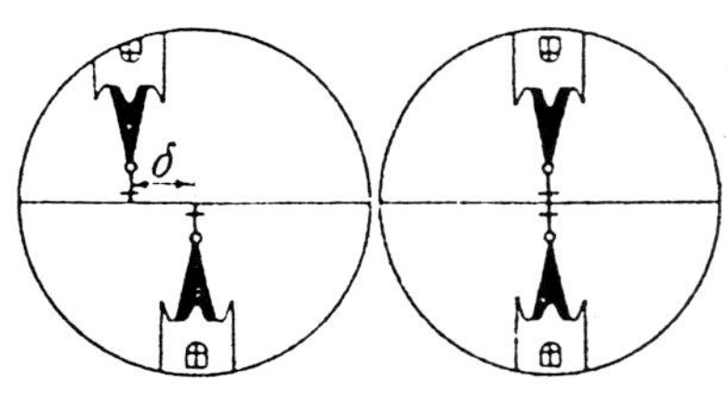

optical function within the device is not within the scope of this book. However, this type of range plotting required that the rangefinding crewman have the ability to visually scan the skies, which not all people necessarily have.

In 1934 the Em 4m R(H) 34 stereoscopic range finder was developed for the heavy Flak. It had an effective range of 670 m to 50,000 m. The subsequent Em 4m R(H) 36 in 1936 could plot targets from 620 m to 50,000 m.

Its 12x magnification could be stepped up to 24x. Another switch allowed the device to switch from range finder to heightfinder and back. Values on the scale were measured in hectometers. The Em 4m R(H) 34 weighed 206 kg, with housing 458 kg. The Em 4m R(H) 36, on the other hand 175 kg, with housing 427 kg. Outside thermal or mechanical influences could cause changes to the system's optics, which could be effectively countered through the aid of a preactivated compensation device.

The improved Em 4m R(H) 40, which appeared in 1940, was not susceptible to such influences, dispensing with the need for any type of special compensation device. The Em 4m R(H) 40 had an effective range of 1,200 m to 100,000 m. With the aid of path speed control the synchronization of calibration marks was activated electrically by a calibration dial, enabling a more accurate calculation of the range. Magnification could be stepped from 20x to 32x. Without its sighting optics and counterbalance the range finder weighed 220 kg; with housing and its balance it weighed 487 kg.

During the Second World War a few 128 mm flak batteries operated the Em 6 stereoscopic range finder (introduced into the Kriegsmarine) in order to acquire targets at even greater ranges.

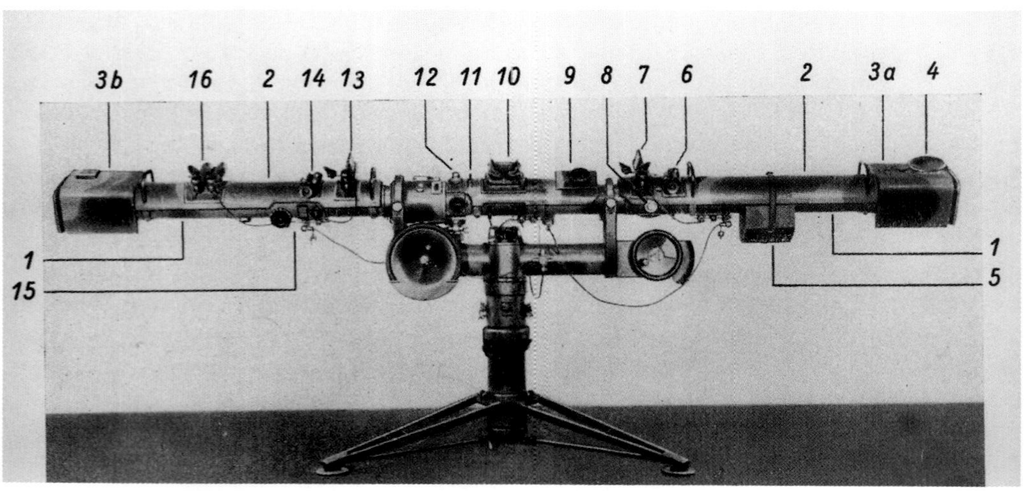

Left: Em 4m R(H) 34 and 36, from viewfinder side. 1) outer tube, 2) protective cover, 3a,3b) left and right base end caps, 4) cover for the heightfinder located on the side, 5) eyepiece cover, 6) removeable search telescope (right), 7) removeable, single lens telescopic sight (right), 8) range collimator, 9) calibration dial, 10) range finder viewer, 11) coarse sight, 12) elevation collimator, 13) removeable, single lens telescopic sight (left), 14) removeable search telescope (left), 15) switch from range finder to heightfinder, 16) removeable, double lens observation scope (from 2nd Dv.T. 1300, picture 1)

Left: An Em 4m R(H) 36, set up on its pedestal base, with the large elevation adjustment wheel on the left and the somewhat smaller wheel for adjusting the traverse on the right.

Right: Opposite side of an Em 4m R(H) 34 or 36, which was part of a Kommandohilfsgerät 35 auxiliary fire director. In addition to the range finder crewman (center) and the two sighting crewmen, the B4 is also standing next to the device (left). His job was to pass the plotted ranges or altitudes by radio to the fire control system.

Right: The twin optics can be seen clearly on this Em 4m R40. The holders for the four 2B38 batteries hang from the pedestal base. These were wired in series and had an output of 4 volts at 76 amps.

Below: This Em 6m R is set up at a Kriegsmarine range finder's school, where these students are conducting ranging exercises.

Above: Various range finders have been set up at a Kriegsmarine range finder's school training site. Notice that on the Em 6m the sighting crew stands and the range finder operator sits and revolve with the system.

Range finder WITH FIRE CONTROL COMPUTER (Kdo.Re.)

Up until around 1936/37 the heavy Flak used the fire control computer (Kommandorechner, or Kdo.Re.) to determine firing values. This computer was attached to an Em 4m R(H). After the E2 and E3 sight operators determined a target's height and bearing, the E1 could plot its range (when determining elevation the altitude was determined to the present position of the target), which was read off by the B4 and called out to the B5. The B5 in turn entered the data on the range scale of the Kdo.Re. The B6 passed the deflection angle read from the azimuth scale and the B7 the elevation (to the target's present position) by radio to the guns. Using this data these guns then sighted in on the target with their direct sighting telescopes. Once this had occurred and "target acquired" had been passed back to the Kdo.Re., the computer provided continuous updates of lead deflection angle (slide rule) and lead elevation angle (automatic corrector + tangent sight) back to the guns, wher the K8 and K9 crewmen used the information to adjust their AAA direct sighting telescopes. At the Kdo.Re. the B8 continuously read off the fuze settings in degrees from the crosshairs on the fuze scale and passed them by radio to the K6 at the guns.

It's probably obvious that, with the increasing speeds of airborne targets, firing with the Kdo.Re. was becoming less and less successful. The lag time between Kdo.Re. and guns was much too long and the potential for errors was too great. Significantly better results were being achieved with the fire control systems which had been tested and put into operation in the meantime.

This sketch shows an Em 4m with fire control computer and crew stations.

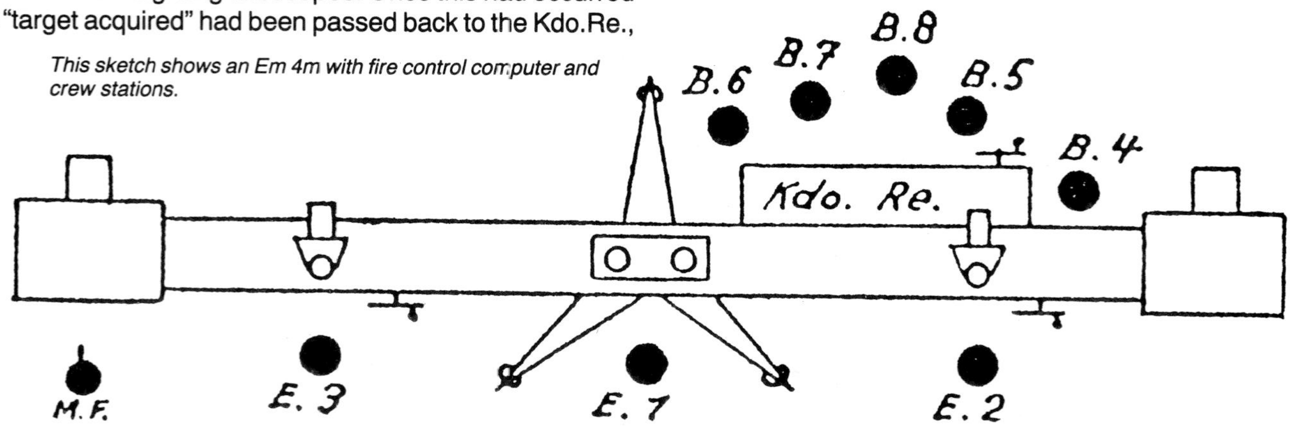

KOMMANDOHILFSGERÄT 35 (KDO.HI. 35) AUXILIARY FIRE DIRECTOR

The Kommandohilfsgerät 35 auxiliary fire director was developed in the years 1930-1935 and saw front line service from 1935 onward. Range finder and fire director, which had its own sight, were set up separately. Values for firing azimuth, total elevation and fuze settings, which were passed to the guns via radio, were determined by the angular velocity method. I.e. an approach solution for the lead factor was attained by multiplying the rate of change to the angle of approach with the (erroneous) projectile flight time to the target's current position. The calculations were made by using friction gears, ballistic cams and tachometers. Due to limited space, a description of the mechanical operation involved in making these calculations is not possible here.

When determining firing values the Kdo.Hi.Ger. 35 system took into account a load delay time of 3 seconds, the sum of all interior ballistic factors, i.e. changes to the Vo by the standard velocity error factor, barrel pressure, powder temperature and air density as well as drift due to the spin of the projectile. Factors which could not be taken into account with the system were wind influence and a horizontal and vertical differences in the gun positions. It therefore always had to be sited in the center of the battery, which naturally increased the crew's difficulties in combat situations. On the other hand, it had the advantage of not requiring an energy source since all data was determined by mechanical means. Only the power needed to pass data from the range finder to the fire control system and from there to the guns came from a battery, which was attached to a brace on the range finder.

When set up, the system was supported by a mount on a tripod. When being transported in a Sonderanhänger 53 single-axle trailer it was bolted down to a carrier bed, then set on the trailer's carrier frame and slid into the trailer by a rail.

The device weighed 156 kg minus accessories, the support frame 65 kg, the tripod 24 kg and the accessories box and contents 30.55 kg. The range finder required a four-man crew, while the control system need nine men and a commander.

The troops didn't particularly like the system, in part due to its inaccuracies when determining firing values (although these were for the most part due to operator error) but primarily because of errors which crept in when passing data by radio. The auxiliary fire director was therefore relegated to Befehlsstelle II, or secondary command post, and was only used when the primary command post's Kdo.Ger. 36 or Kdo.Ger. 40 wasn't operating.

Below: This Kommandohilfsgerät 35 with its attendant Em 4m R(H) 34 or 36 was photographed on 21 June 1940 at a site near Sprendlingen.

Above: The covered Kdo.Hi.Ger. 35 rests with its carrier bed on the extended carrier frame of the Sonderanhänger 53 trailer (Sd.Ah. 53).

Above: The Sd.Ah. 53 for the Kdo.Hi.Ger. 35 with the carrier frame pulled out. The fire controller device on its bed is in the foreground.

Below: The carrier arms on this auxiliary fire controller have not yet been pushed in, although the panoramic scope for calibrating the system with the guns has already been attached.

Below: the Kdo.Hi.Ger. 35 on its tripod mount is seen here hidden beneath its protective cover.

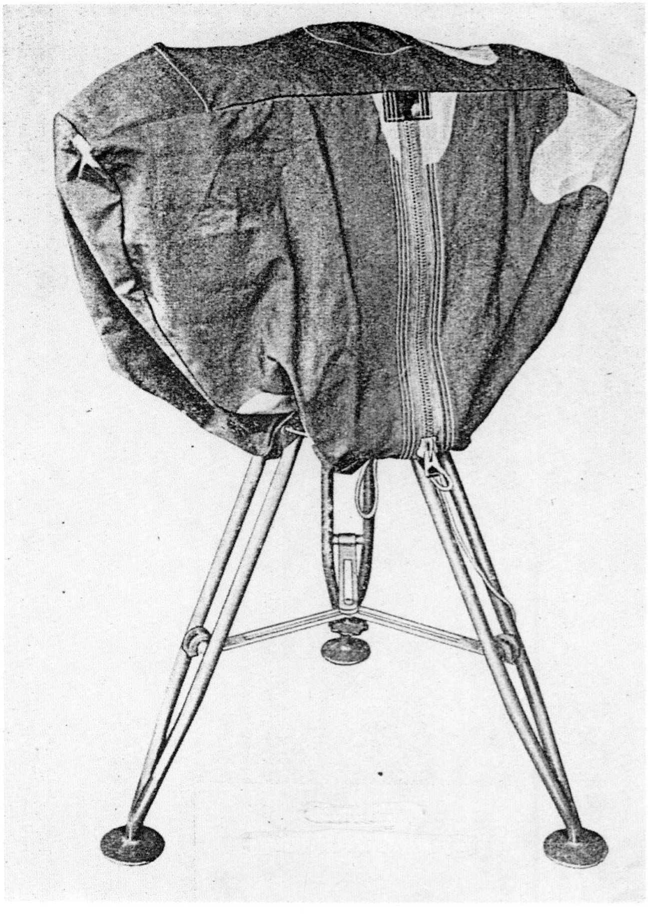

Right: Markings for the impact azimuth, lead azimuth and a scale for the instant of azimuth determination can be seen on the backside of the Kdo.Hi.Ger. 35. Above the latter is the tachometer for the lead azimuth; left of that is the adjusting knob for making corrections to the lead azimuth and another for drift correction. To the right of the tachometer is the adjusting knob for lead azimuth, above which is the coarse switch for the azimuth and next to the equipment number (458) is the switch for signaling when target has been acquired. Also visible are the brake knobs on the left for azimuth rate and on the right for elevation rate.

Below: This photo shows the device from the right side with elevation adjusting scope and the elevation sighting operator, the B6. He is operating the handwheel for plotting the angle of elevation to the target at the instant of range determination. Beneath the marks for barrel elevation, lead elevation, angle of elevation and instant of elevation determination is the wheel with a lock grip for lead elevation. The elevation tachometer is above this and to the right. Next to that is the adjusting knob for making corrections to the lead elevation. Beneath this is the right level gauge under glass.

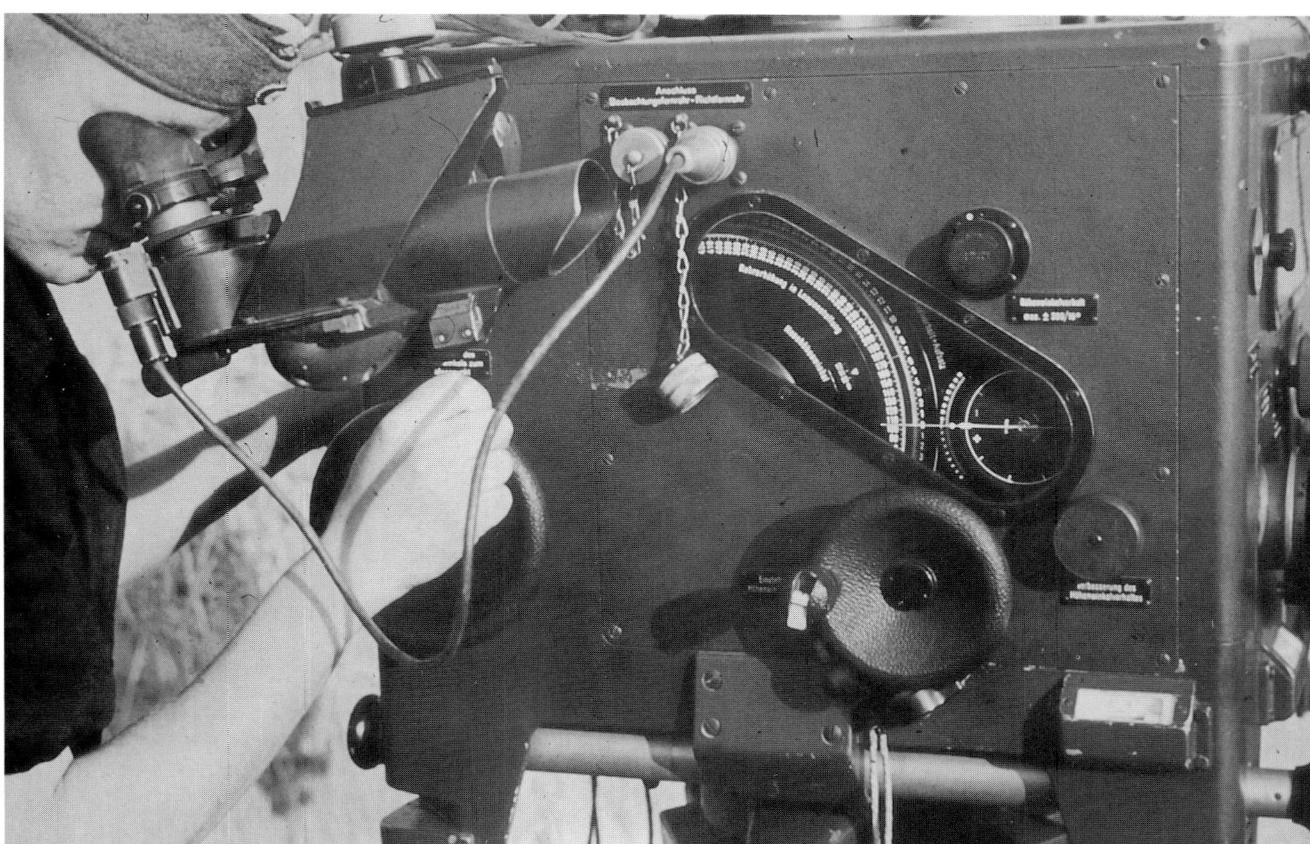

Above: The front panel contains the range drum with kurvengleicher target range and gleicher target altitude, plus the counters for target's current range and impact range located above the drum. The tachometer below shows the range fluctuation speed. To the left of this is the adjusting knob for making corrections to the summ of all interior ballistic factors, while below that is the handwheel with lockgrip and locking lever for the range fluctuation speed. The B7 used the larger handwheel on the right for inputting the target's current range passed by the B4 at the range finder. Using the lever on the handwheel's grip, the overdrive for this could be switched on. The second bubble level was also for levelling the system.

Below: This photo shows the device from the left side with the lateral adjusting telescope and its power drive motor, operated by the B5. The B13 read off the fuze status from the large scale in the center of this side of the system and passed this off by radio to the guns. Using the knob to the left of the fuze scale, modifications could be made to the fuze status based on load delay time, the data for which could be read off above the fuze scale. The two small drums showed the current and impact ranges. The range fluctuation speed could be frozen with the aid of the knob to the left and below.

Right: The Kdo.Hi.Ger. 35 inside a Sd.Ah. 53, towed by the standard vehicle for carrying Flak trackers, the Kfz. 24 (here with all crewmembers seated). The box for the Em 4m R(H) is in the cargo bed, topped by the box for the collimator and the tied-down base mount.

The drawing on the right shows the crew stations for the Kdo.Hi.Ger. 35 with Em 4m R(H): E1 height-finder sergeant, E2 lateral tracker, E3 elevation tracker, B4 passed data via voice radio to the B7, B5 controlled the computer laterally, B6 controlled it vertically. Speed of revolution, controlled by the adjusting gears, corresponded to the azimuth and elevation lead. The azimuth lead was passed by the B8, who kept the pointer on the azimuth tachometer aligned with the null marker; the B9 did the same for the elevation tachometer. The B10 passed the range lead using the range fluctuation speed tachometer. The B11 gave the firing azimuth, the B12 the barrel elevation and the B13 the fuze setting by voice radio to the guns.

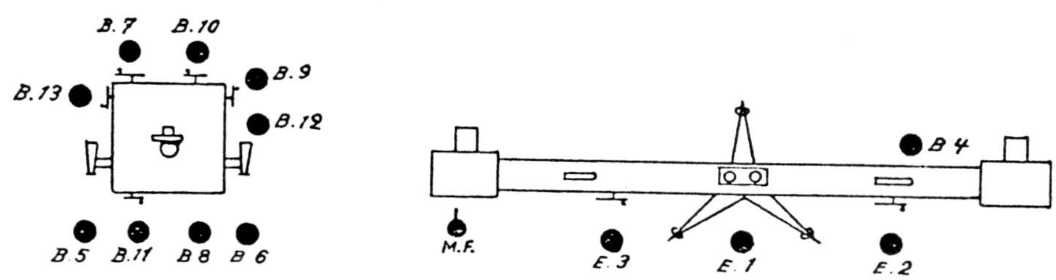

Below: Training being carried out on a Kdo.Hi.Ger. 35 in a well laid-out site for a 88 mm AAA battery.

Left: Even railroad AAA units were sometimes equipped with the Kdo.Hi.Ger. 35. The Em 4m R(H) and the computer were located together on a flatcar. To give the crew more room to operate the flatcar's sideboards could be folded down horizontally.

Below: This photo shows how the auxiliary fire controller is anchored to the floor of the flatcar. One of the two air observers is standing behind the searchlight controller optics. In the foreground on the left is part of the collimator for the Em 4m R(H). This railroad AAA battery was probably operating in Russia at the time this picture was taken, since on the flatcar's right sideboard can be seen hand grenades close at hand for defense against partisan attacks.

Below: Taken on a VOMAG vehicle of Befehlsstelle II, a battery of I/42(mot.S.) is seen here during a stop on 10 May 1941 on the way to Bremen. Only the Em 4m R(H) of the auxiliary fire control system can be seen. The 88 mm AAA guns and fire control systems of this unit were mounted on the lower floorboards of busses built by the Vogtländische Maschinenfabrik AG (VOMAG). The vehicles' six-cylinder diesel engines, type VOMAG 6R 3080, had an output of 150 hp.

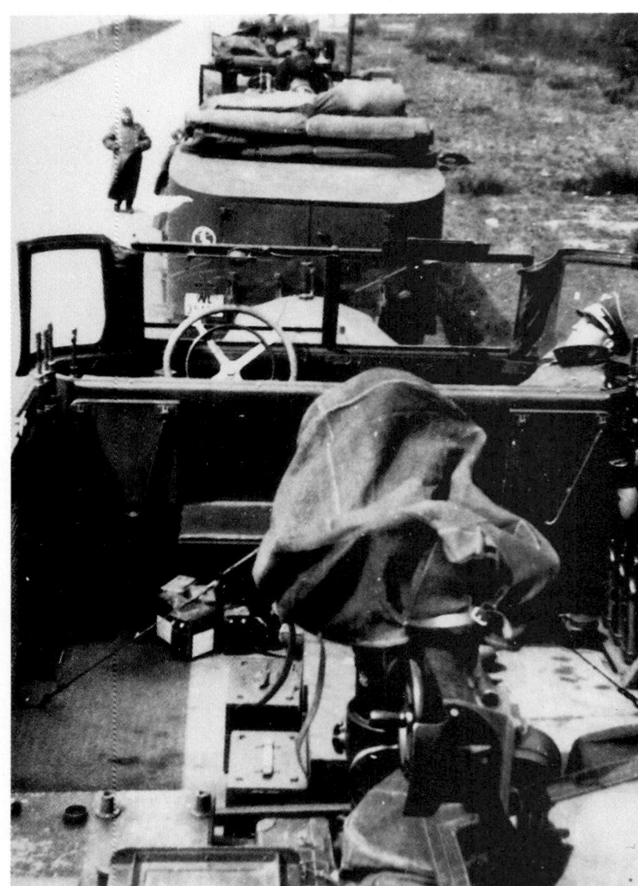

KOMMANDOGERÄT 36 (KDO.GER. 36) FIRE CONTROL SYSTEM

As was mentioned earlier, Geheimrat (First Counselor) Pschorr had developed a fire control system during the First World War which, due to various reasons, was never used operationally. After restrictions on development of AAA weapons and related systems, brought about by the Treaty of Versailles, had been relaxed, the first prototype of the "Kommandogerät Pschorr 27" underwent testing. The range finder on this variant was still a separate piece. Unlike the Kdo.Hi.Ger. 35, Pschorr's device worked on the linear plotting principle by portraying a scaled-down geometric pattern of the target's movement on the map surface.

After a few significant changes and improvements the system was supplied to the front line troops in 1936 as the Kommandogerät 36. The Em 4m R(H) range finder rested on top of the computer, so that plot values for azimuth, elevation and range could be automatically fed into the computer. The computer, in turn, plotted the firing values for total elevation, firing azimuth and fuze delay time for the point of detonation based on provided direction of flight, target speed and the projectile's flight time to impact point. Factored into this equation were the command and load delay times, as a rule three seconds, as well as the particular ballistic and weather influences. These included:

1) Barrel condition of the guns, which varied based on the number of rounds fired. Deviations from the firing table values were determined by V0 firing, needed from time to time, and incorporated into the base factor used to compensate for velocity error
2) Projectile weight class
3) Powder temperature and powder dampness; both were measured several times daily in a charge temperature cartridge at the ammunition dump
4) Projectile drift
5) Air density, which according to the firing table data used the base of 1.22 kg/m³
6) Wind speed
7) Wind direction

In order to compensate for the latter three weather factors, each battery received a weather report several times each day, the data from which was entered into the fire controller's wind analyzer and parallax offset mechanism.

Since both a horizontal and vertical siting differential between system and the center of the gun battery could be compensated for the system could be set up 300 - 500 m from the gun battery. As with the Kdo.Ger. 35, this permitted the crew to carry out their duties uninterrupted by the firing guns.

The range finder required three crewmen to operate, while the computer needed ten men and a commander.

Firing values for azimuth, elevation and fuze delay time were relayed to the guns' signal receivers by three transmitters at the fire controller via landline or, when this was not operating (which only happened very rarely), passed by voice radio.

Without its range finder the Kdo.Ger. 36 weighed 975 kg, on its base 1,375 kg and with two-axled Sonderanhänger 104 trailer and base 2,952 kg.

Improvements were constantly being made to the system. As an example, it was discovered shortly after the war broke out that a few of the coverage areas were not adequate. Accordingly, the plotting capability for horizontal target speed was increased from 150 m/s (540 kmh) to 180 m/s (648 kmh), while vertical speed was boosted from 60 m/s to 120 m/s. In addition, the map range to the target's plotted position was increased from 13,000 m to 15,000 m and map range for point of impact from 10,000 m to 13,000 m. On the other hand, the lateral range of movement for the system remained limited to 2 x 360 to either side.

This photo shows the front side of a Kdo.Ger. 36, which has been set up somewhere in the East. Notice the two support arms with their ball-shaped white knobs, which served as supports for the protective tarpaulin when the device was being transported and were normally removed when the system was set up for operations.

Left: This is the rear view of a Kdo.Ger. 36 minus its range finder. It was only on the Kdo.Ger. 36 that the handwheels for the angular height (502, operated by the E3, right) and azimuth (510 slow, 511 rapid, operated by the E2, left) at instant of range determination could be found. Both operators stood on either side of the height-finder sergeant, the E1. If the E2 were incapacitated the E3 could also pivot the system laterally using the auxiliary crank (512). 78, 95 and 98 are cover hatches; 3 and 5 are also cover hatches behind which is located the warning alarm which sounded after the system had made two 360° rotations in either direction. In addition, this limitation was also notated on a warning plate (91). 77 was the "free running" activation switch for lateral movement, 97 the drive housing for the lateral control power drive, 150 the elevation housing, 395 the cover to the Vh spring mechanism, and 8 was the hand coupler disk for the range finder with a red lineup mark. (From L.Dv.T. 1350/2, which remarkably identifies this side of the system as the front, whereas all other descriptions of range finders and fire control systems call the side on which the trackers look into the optics the back.)

The photo below shows the front side of the system with the handwheel for barrel elevation (505), the barrel elevation drum located above that (124, right), the electric scales for the ballistic drum (118) and its cover. Located in the center of the system are the adjusting knobs for fuze corrections (107), for projectile spin and azimuth corrections (108) and for barrel elevation corrections (109). Below these are the firing value indicators for barrel elevation (351), transmitter for barrel elevation (121), cover with countersunk screws (52) for the load delay multiplier (51), four-cornered shaft for adjusting the load delay time, transmitter (122) and gauge (350) for the fuze delay time, handwheel (504) for passing the fuze delay time with fuze drum (124, left), electro-technical gauge (115) and graduation (119) for the fuze drum, socket head cap screws for the correction device (126) and handwheel for horizontal velocity (503). (From L.Dv.T. 1350/2, diagram 4)

Above: This Kdo.Ger. 36 served with the 1/407, a 105 mm AAA battery, in Büderich near Düsseldorf in 1940.

Right: This sketch shows the crew positions of a Kdo.Ger. 36 during operations. The E1 at the Em 4m R(H) passes range; the E2 tracks the target horizontally, while the E3 tracks the target vertically. The B11 constantly reads off the tracking figures and calls these out to the B4 and B5 as "elevation tracking", while quietly passing "range tracking" to the B5 only. The B4 stands at the elevation housing and there passes the vertical speed and lead elevation, while the B5 follows the calls by the B11 using a handwheel to move the electro-mechanical pointer along the black elevation curve when plotting altitude and along the red distance curve when plotting range. At the path-of-flight recorder, the B6 reports the direction and speed of the target. The B7 turns on the electric motor and, using one handwheel, passes the azimuth lead, while with another he operates the pointer on the radius vector arm. The B8 adjusts the barrel elevation drum with a handwheel based on the elevation curve plots, and the B9 does the same for the pointer on the fuze setting drum. The B10 works at the correction controls, the B13 calls out corrections to the ballistic wind analysis data to the B10 and the B12 mans the power switchbox. (From L.Dv 400/4a)

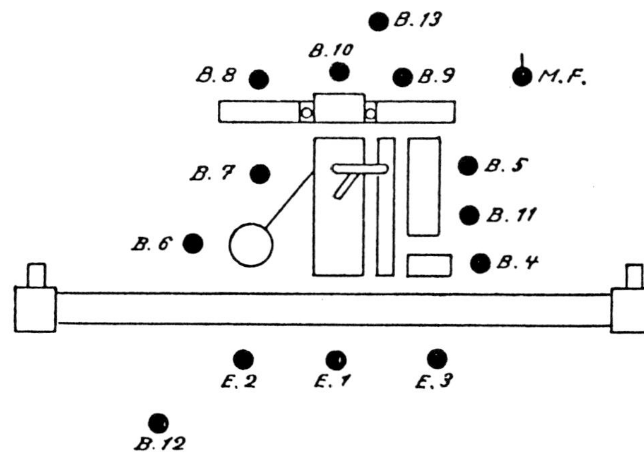

Below: The crew of a Kdo.Ger. 36 stand at their post. At the far right the battery commander monitors the air situation with his binoculars, while in front of him the plotting officer has telephoned the guns. The tracking team commander, here an NCO, stands in the foreground and monitors the crew's work.

Left: The path-of-flight plotting table (117) and its plotting stylus was located on the system's left side, while above that was the graphical speed display. The round gauge next to this is the speed reference dial, with the large handwheel (133) for determining the target's horizontal velocity below. Also shown are the handcrank (195) for lateral lead, the path-of-flight arm with panoramic scope housing case (144) and base (143) above that, and the Em 4m R(H) 34 or 36 (225) with its two mounting collars (141). On the base's cross supports (243) can be seen four trunnions (244), four locking travel hooks (246) for the Sonderanhänger 104 trailer as well as three leveling mechanisms (247) with hand cranks and footplates. (From L.Dv.T. 1350/1, diagram 12)

Left: This crew of a Kdo.Ger. 36 has fallen out for an inspection by the regimental commander.

Left: The B6 at work on the path-of-flight plotting table. This was a sheet of matte glass onto which the target's path was projected onto a fixed underlying map in reduced scale using a recording stylus. In order to relay the direction of flight, the B6 had to use the handwheel for target direction to trace the target's path with the red-green lines on the plotting table. In addition, he reported the target's horizontal speed by using the handwheel for horizontal speed (upper photo, no. 133) and mirroring the parallel lines on the "graphical speed indicator" with the lines showing up here.

Right: The right side of the system with the electro-mechanical drum (33), the protective housing (25) and the handcrank for the electro-mechanical slide (500). To the left of the elevation box can be seen the large handwheel for the plotted elevation angle at the instant of range determination (502), while on the elevation box itself is the knob for setting the perpendicular distance between the fire control system and the firing battery (514). Also visible are the handcrank for the elevation lead (516), the handcrank for the target's present altitude (517) and the handcrank for powered or manual operation of the vertical speed and elevation control to the target's current position (518). (From L.Dv.T. 1350/2, diagram 2)

Right: Overall view of a Kdo.Ger. 36 in position, seen from the front right quarter with the elevation box, the large electro-mechanical drum, the fine adjustment knobs and the drums for determining fuze delay time and barrel elevation.

Right: The sighting crewmen track the departing aircraft with their optics. The other crewmembers have broken off their activities. Note the sighting scopes for the E2 and E3 on this Em 4m R(H). These are the 10x80 twin scopes from a Scheinwerferrichtungsweiser 35 with the typical auxiliary sights above, which enables a backwards facing second observer to follow the instructions of the aimer.

Above: I Abteilung of Flakregiment 42 (mot.S.) was the sole AAA regiment in the German Wehrmacht equipped with VOMAG lowboy trucks. The four 88 mm guns as well as the Kdo.Hi.Ger. 35 and Kdo.Ger. 36 for each of the three (later four) batteries were carried on these VOMAG vehicles. Above we see the Kdo.Ger. 36 on the plotting vehicle of Befehlsstelle I of 2 Batterie.

Left: This photo shows the plotting vehicle for Befehlsstelle I with the Kdo.Ger. 36 of 2 Batterie of I/42 (mot.S.) at the Führer headquarters "Süd" (South), approximately 120 km east of Krakow on 23 September 1941.

Left: Yet another picture from 2 Batterie of I/42 (mot.S.) in position near Stettin in October of 1941. The vehicle in the foreground is the plotting vehicle for Befehlsstelle I with the Kdo.Ger. 36. The vehicle's sideboards have been lowered to increase the platform operating area. Unlike the gun vehicles, the plotting vehicles could also be accessed from the rear in order to be able to load the Em 4m R(H) and collimator.

Right: Three air observers have been assigned to this Kdo.Ger. 36 for scanning the skies. This indicates that it was seldom possible to expect any kind of advance warning. The battery was alerted to approaching enemy aircraft by a hand siren, which can be seen here between the two observers on the left. The clear field of view from the device out to the sea leads one to believe that this gun battery was also employed to attack ocean going targets.

Right: Judging by the landscape, this Kdo.Ger. 36 is sited in northern Russia. The collimator for the Em 4m R(H) is on the protective embankment.

Right: The boxes with the Em 4m R(H) and its associated collimator with base mount have already been unloaded from the rangefinding team's vehicle, a Kfz. 74. The distributor box follows. A line drum, also called a cable drum, hangs from the driver's cab. Below that, a cable cart could be loaded/unloaded from the area accessed by the open side hatch cover.

Above: This temporary position in the middle of a sunflower field has been protected by hastily woven fascines.

Below: The "technical firing" operator observes the target through his twin optics. In addition, the B6 can be seen working at the path-of-flight plotter.

Below: Alert for a Kdo.Ger. 36 crew. With the lateral power drive shut off, the system is manually swung around to face the target. This position is well laid out and is protected by a blast wall made of sandbags.

Above: Another overall view of a Kdo.Ger. 36. The two cross supports can be seen to good advantage in this photo, as can two of the three leveling spindles and the hooks with which the system is attached to the two carriages of the Sd.Ah. 104 trailer.

Below: Alert at a railway AAA battery. The Kdo.Ger. 36 crewmen race from their barracks wagon to the system, which is set up on a special flatbed car. The sideboards (which could be folded horizontally for expanding the platform area) hold the boxes for the Em 4m R(H) and collimator. Unusual for a railway AAA battery, the Sd.Ah. 104 here is being carried on the railcar together with the system itself.

KOMMANDOGERÄt 40 (KDO.GER. 40) FIRE CONTROL SYSTEM

By 1937 the Carl Zeiss, Jena Company was already at work on a AAA fire control system which operated on a linear geometric basis and which could carry out the necessary computations virtually automatically, thereby eliminating human error. Even altitude and course changes of the target being engaged could be taken into account when computing the firing values. Such a system required highly refined drive units and servo-motors in the shape of ballistic cams, differentials, friction gears, governors and switch boxes, all driving 20 electro-motors.

In 1940 this new Kommandogerät 40 began appearing in front line units, where it was initially called the "Kappa" device. Named for the Greek letter Kappa, which was used to designate the azimuth of the target and which played a major role in the system's calculations.

The Kdo.Ger. 40's computer was linked with the stereoscopic Em 4m R40 range finder or the older Em 4m R(H) 34/36, so that the plotted azimuth, elevation and range of the target's current position could be fed directly into the computer.

In order to permit a smooth lateral and vertical control, the adjusting handwheels moved a path-speed drive, by which the change in angular velocities of a target flying a straight path could be automatically plotted.

The system was crewed by a squad leader, three crewmen on the Em 4m R40, two on the computer and one on the Maschinensatz 50V (-), 1.5 kW 30 power supply and batteries with switchbox.

Three batteries with 36 volts supplied the system with electricity. There was a power generator providing 1.5 kW and 50 volts available when the batteries needed recharging or for continuous floating battery operations. As with the Kdo.Ger. 36 the firing values were passed to the guns by means of either a Lampenübertragungsgerät 30 illuminated data transfer system or via the Übertragungsgerät 37 alternating current follow-the-pointer data transmission system.

The system was portable using the single-axle Sonderanhänger 52 trailer. The box with the Em 4m R40 and all accessories, plus batteries, power generator, cable drums, cable cart, crates with the sighting scopes were packed onto the Meßkw. 74 or the 8-ton Zgkw. Kfz 7/6 prime mover. In order to facilitate easier loading of the 427 kg crate with the Em 4m R40, both vehicles had rails which could be pulled out from the cargo bed's center, on which the crates could be pushed up onto the bed on rollers.

Ranges and Weights for the Kdo.Ger. 40.
Ranges:
unlimited horizontal sweep coverage
plotted angular height - 0° to 90°
slant range to target - 1,200 m to 18,000 m
plotted target altitude - 0 to 11,800 m
map range to impact point - 800 to 14,500 m
impact altitude - 0 to 11,800 m
horizontal target speed - 0 to 300 m/s

Weights:
Em 4m R40 including sighting scopes - 195 kg
Kdo.Ger. 40 in travel mode - 2,260 kg
Kdo.Ger. 40 in position - 1,595 kg
Trailer - 2,860 kg

Below: The Kommandogerät 40 (Kdo.Ger. 40) on the Sd.Ah. 52 with a Kabeltrommel 30 cable drum, onto which the 108-wire Übertragungsleitung 30 data transmission cable for the Lampenübertragungsgerät 30 is wound.

The following marked photographs come from the first system types from the "provisional description of the Kdo.Ger. 40" pamphlet (Vorläufige Beschreibung des Kdo.Ger. 40), published in 1940. Later systems had changes made to the configuration of some of their gauges, r/t connections and switches.

Right: This is the rear view of the Kdo.Ger. 40 minus range finder with (34) trihedral and pointer (35) for switching off the device's lateral movement when sighting, mount (33) and trihedral crank (36), switch for range finder illumination (42), travel stand for the E1 (32), fuze box containing 21 fuzes for the electro-motors (39), and amperemeter (38). (From Vorläufige Beschreibung des Kdo.Ger. 40, part I, diagram 16)

Right:

This system was part of the Wehrtechnische Studiensammlung in Coblenz, but has currently been removed from display for restoration. The Em 4m R40 is missing the lateral and vertical sighting optics as well as the counterbalances for these optics. Notice the receiver box with the receivers for the Folgezeigerübertragungsgerät 37 for the plotted values for range, azimuth and altitude, which has been "borrowed" for the fire control system from a radar set.

Right: This photo shows the rear view of the same system with the viewscope for the E1. To the right is the plotting wheel and the switch knobs for polarized glass and magnification. On the viewscope's left is the adjusting knob for "precise altitude", plus the knob and switch for illuminating the track. The handwheel with slip catch for feeding in the range-to-target plot is in the center of the device. Also visible are the gauges with the follow-the-pointers on the receiver box (given the macabre nickname of "child's coffin" by the troops) for the input data from the radar system, with the receiver for the target's plotted altitude on the left. The range-to-target plot receiver is in the center and to the right is the receiver for the target's plotted azimuth. Since the illuminated markings on the scales give off radioactive rays, the warning stickers seen here were applied after the war.

Above: Notice on this, the system's left side, the handwheel for azimuth path plotter (191), the handwheel for determining the vertical angle to the target's plotted position (197) with handgrip (198) and slip catch (199). The gauges for the target lateral lead (192), the azimuth of target (193), projectile flight time (194, dropped on later models), azimuth to target's plotted position (195), horizontal leg between present and future positions (196), firing barrel elevation (201), angle of elevation to plotted position (202), range to plotted position (203), map range to point of impact (211) and altitude to point of impact were all photographically recorded during simulated firing in order to be able to evaluate the results both by computer and by hand. (From Vorläufige Beschreibung des Kdo.Ger. 40, part I, diagram 17)

Below: The gauge for the firing azimuth (35) can be seen in the center of the front panel. Left and above are the adjusting knobs for ballistic factors, wind direction and wind speed; these were later all replaced by trihedrals. (From Vorläufige Beschreibung des Kdo.Ger. 40, part I, diagram 15)

Right: The crew of a Kdo.Ger. 40, here during an evaluation on optical usage. To the directional controller's left in the foreground can be seen one of the AAA recording cameras necessary for such evaluations. The system in the background is a Kdo.Ger. 36 in position. The two axle frames of its Sd.Ah. 104 have been parked next to a shed.

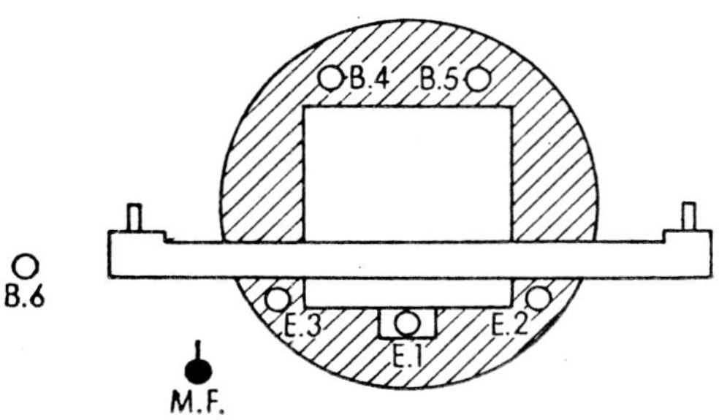

Above: The drawing and the two photos show the crew positions on a Kdo.Ger. 40 in position. E1 - range finder, E2 - azimuth tracker and E3 - elevation tracker. The B4 determined the manual course, in which he first moved the aircraft figure on the system's topside in the direction of the folded out indicator signal by turning the handwheel for the azimuth path plotter and then turned the handwheel again so that the last marked curve section on the azimuth path plotter overlayed a curve on the curvelinear cylinder drum. When the altitude changed, he switched from "manual course" to "automatic course". The B5 operated the main switch, the switches for "ranging normal", "last altitude stands", "course stands" and "target turning", as well as the tachometer for determining the horizontal speed, the Vh. The B6 ran the Maschinensatz 1.5 kW 50V and the power switch box.

Right: Visible here on the system's topside is the elongated glass plate for the azimuth track plotter in front of the B4 with cylinder drum. Above this is the round indicator signal screen for aircraft direction, wind direction and direction of the perpendicular distance between the fire control system and the gun battery.

Left: Befehlsstelle I's station showing a Kdo.Ger. 40 of 1/407 in Düsseldorf-Mörsenbroich following an American bombing raid on 5 January 1944, during which the Luftwaffe auxiliary troops seen here also suffered losses.

Below: Beneath the lateral driver on this Kdo.Ger. 40 can be seen the opening into which an acetylene lamp was place to heat the system in winter. The device in the foreground is a switch box belonging to a Maschinensatz 50V(-) 1.5 kW 30 power generator.

Below: Luftwaffe auxiliary troops operating a Kdo.Ger. 40. The Hitler Youth armbands were only worn with reluctance and, despite orders to the contrary, were usually taken off when on leave; the young men viewed themselves as soldiers, not just Hitler Youth.

Above: This Kdo.Ger. 40 was sited on top of the fire control tower in Hamburg-Heiligengeistfeld.

Flak towers were built to provide better protection for the city centers of Hamburg, Berlin and Vienna, and were armed with heavy AAA guns. They had a supplemental role of providing citizens with air raid shelters. In addition to those gun towers (G-Türme) with their 105 mm, 128 mm or twin 128 mm AAA guns, there was generally also a fire control tower (L-Turm), on which the fire control and radar systems were situated and the battery commander had his fire control post. The 414(T), eventually equipped with four 128 mm twin AAA guns, was stationed in Hamburg's Heiligengeistfeld, with the G-Turm in the Feldstraße and the L-Turm in the Eimsbütteler Straße. The 123rd Turmflakabteilung's batteries were located in the high-rise bunkers in Berlin: at the zoo, in Friedrichshain and in Humbolthain. In Vienna the tower in Arenbergpark was initially occupied by a 105 mm battery. Following this, the 1/184, a 128 mm twin AAA battery, was stationed there. Also equipped with 128 mm twin guns, the 3/184 was stationed in the tower at Augarten. The photo on the right shows the Kdo.Ger. 40 on the G-Turm in Berlin-Humbolthain, while behind this is one of the four 128 mm twin AAA guns.

Left: A view of the flatcar for a railcar AAA battery, showing the Kdo.Ger. 40. The Em 4m R(H) 34/36 is attached to the fire controller. The collimator is on the right, on the folded down sideboard of the flatcar. The storage compartment behind the fire control system contains the batteries with switchbox. In front of these, hanging from both sides of the walls, are the cable drums with rolled-up Übertragungsleitung 30 data transmission cables.

Left: Cables lead from the radar system via a girder to the follow-the-pointer receiver of the Kdo.Ger. 40 at a railcar AAA battery. The data transmission cable to the guns passes through the flatbed car flooring below right. Since the frame, which acts as the baseplate, could not be increased further, the binocular optics for the "technical firing" crewman is affixed to the range finder beneath its horizontal base.

Left: This is an interesting combination of systems on Befehlsstelle I's flatcar of a railcar AAA battery. In the foreground, an Em 4m R40 is seen mounted on its stand. Behind this, an aerial observer tracks the target using the binocular optics of the Scheinwerferrichtungsweiser 35, while the crew of the Kdo.Ger. 40 gets about their business. The FuMG 62 Würzburg radar doesn't appear to be participating in the exercise, since it's pointed in an entirely different direction.

In order to determine the training state of a battery without the trouble of deploying it to a firing range, so-called optical evaluations were sometimes conducted. In such cases, the precise range to a target aircraft was determined using two photo recorder theodolites located on a pre-surveyed baseline. One of these was set up with the fire controller. Flak photo recording boxes (as they were called in the Vorläufige Beschreibung des Kdo.Ger. 40, part III, B. Flak-Schmalfilm-Gerät, Berlin 1940) were attached to this one and one at the guns, affixed in front of the various gauges and scales for plotting and firing values. These boxes could be activated simultaneously with the theodolites by a hand button on the timer. By evaluating the data photographed in this manner the target's actual flight path and the theoretical detonation point could be shown both by computer and on paper. This was the case when predicted plot, enemy plot and detonation point overlapped. The camera boxes have been affixed to the fire controllers in the photos above and below left for an optical evaluation. You can see the associated cables for the illumination searchlight and for activating the film boxes.

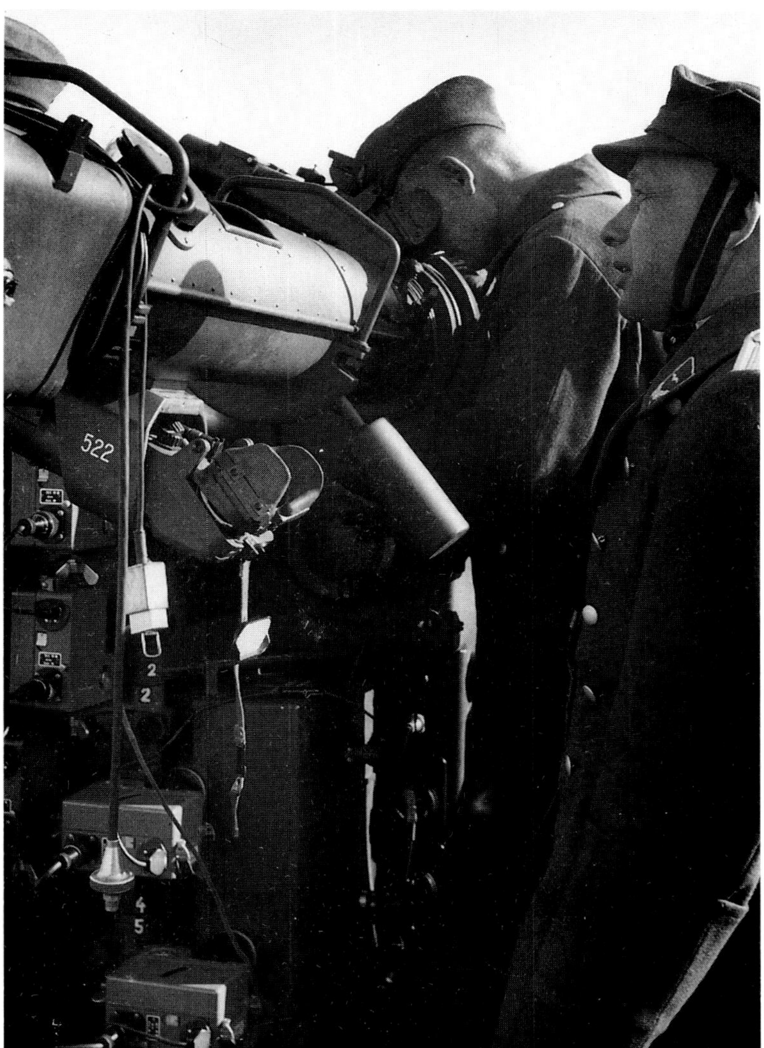

Below: A flak recording box (1) with the lens (2), a Schneider-Xenon (d/f=1:1.5) having a 2.5 cm focal width and a focus range of 14 to 80 cm. The aperature was adjustable from 1.5 to 22. With 36 volts powering the flash (15), illumination time ranged from 1/30 to 1/150 sec., depending on the aperature setting. Power was from a high-speed DC motor having a current of 36 volts. The cassette housed 12 meters of narrow width film (16 mm). A counter showed the current film frame number. (Vorläufige Beschreibung des Kdo.Ger. 40, part III, diagram 1)

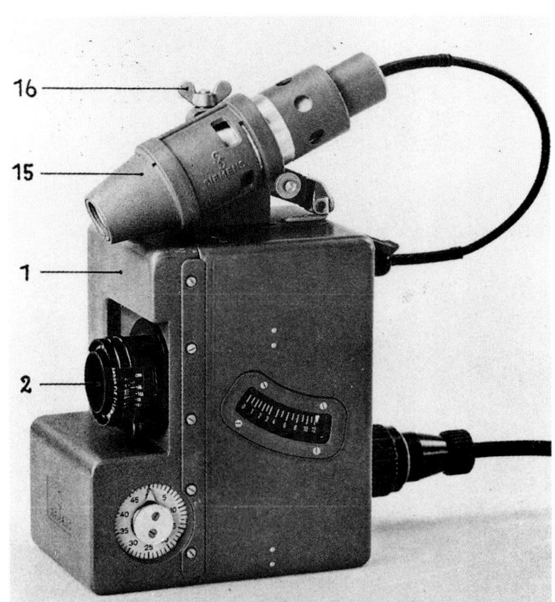

Above: this Kdo.Ger. 40 of 1/407 is set up here for an optical evaluation without flak recording boxes and minus guns; values were written down. Photo was taken in 1940 in the Flakkaserne Hubbeltath near Düsseldorf. The battery with switch box can be seen in the foreground, while in the right of the photo is the stand for one of the two horizontal base theodolites.

Below: Included in the Maschinensatz 50V(-) 1.5 kW 30 field generator was the motor generator, the power switch box, two battery frames (only one shown in photo), the battery charging switch box (not in photo), a 10 m and a 50 m long feed line as well as a protective housing for the motor generator, plus a toolbox and a 20 liter fuel tank. The field generator supplied power to the Kdo.Ger. 40, the communicating devices for command and control operations and the flak recording boxes. When operationally set up, the switch box rested on four feet on top of one of the two battery frames. On top of it, from left to right, were the switches and gauges for data transmitter, fire controller, battery power and voltage meter. The lamp brightness of the receiver, the fire controller power and the generator power during floating battery operation could be regulated using the three handwheels on the frontspiece. The battery frame contains three lead batteries each having 12 volts (Vorläufige Beschreibung des Kdo.Ger. 40, part II, dia. 7)

Right: The motor generator, seen here resting on a battery frame, consisted of an air-cooled two-stroke engine having 3.25 hp at 2000 rpm. It powered a voltage generator, a DC shunt-type generator with an output of 1.5kW at 50 volts. Motor and generator were permanently joined by a coupling. (Vorläufige Beschreibung des Kdo.Ger. 40, part II, dia. 6)

110 cm, 150 cm and 200 cm SEARCHLIGHTS

The use of searchlights (Sw. from the German word Scheinwerfer) for nighttime air defense had been considered even before the First World War, where they were primarily envisioned as countermeasures to the operations of enemy airships. One of the first searchlight exercises using 60 cm and 90 cm field- and fortress searchlights working in conjunction with AAA guns took place near Coblenz in 1913. Since the altitude of the airships was around 1,000 m and their speed was approximately 60 kmh, the searchlights of the day proved effective enough. Up until the beginning of World War I, therefore, improvements to searchlights were deemed unnecessary.

However, shortly after the outbreak of this conflict, it quickly became apparent that enemy air raids increasingly involved significantly faster aircraft flying at night over the front, staging areas and the homeland itself. Since accurate AAA defensive fire was only possible if the target were sighted visually, the numbers and effectiveness of the available field and fortress searchlights were woefully inadequate. Nighttime anti-aircraft defense accordingly often took the form of simply throwing up a barrage fire, the altitude of which was based on the known operating altitudes of approaching aircraft. This required a considerable expenditure of ammunition and was not generally all that successful.

In 1916, therefore, the 110 cm and 200 cm searchlights then in use by the Marine on warships and for coastal protection, respectively, were also employed as AAA searchlights. A stationary base permitted the searchlight to be swiveled horizontally through a full 360°, while the housing could be tipped 90° in the vertical plane. With the aid of a guide rod, one man could move the searchlight both horizontally and vertically. However, the ranges of the 110 cm searchlight (approx. 4,000 m) and the 200 cm searchlight (approx. 5,500 m) did not entirely meet the expectations of the Inspekteur der Flakwaffen. Later, however, their intensity was tripled by making improvements to the lamps.

A 30 hp four-cylinder motor generator served as the power supply, driving a DC dynamo with an output of 16.5 kW and 165 amps. The 110 cm searchlight was mobile, pulled either by horse on a searchlight wagon drawn by a four horse team and followed by a four-horse team generator wagon and two-horse team equipment cart, or motorized on a 3-ton searchlight transport and 3-t generator transport with a two-wheeled equipment cart in tow. It was also permanently mounted on railway cars or in fixed sites.

Below: The 110 cm searchlight with
a) bedplate with lifting jacks
b) base
c) turntable with support arms
d) searchlight housing
e) cable connectors
f) plug for data transmitter
g) lamp elevation data transmitter
h) lamp azimuth data transmitter
i) slip ring for data transmitters
k) graduated circle plate for azimuth
l) graduated arc for elevation
m) elevation handwheel
n) azimuth locking lever
o) gauge
p) guide rod
q) cover glass
r) ventilation chamber
s) lamp
t) reflector
u) diopter
(From VDJ "Flugabwehr)

Only a few examples of the mobile, railcar-mounted version of the 200 cm searchlight were supplied to front-line troops near the end of WWI, by which time 465 110 cm and 25 200 cm searchlights were in operation.

With the rebuilding of the German Wehrmacht from 1935 onward, a handful of these were taken over by the Reichswehr for the flak arm. From this point on, however, only 60 cm searchlights were built new for the light AAA and the newly developed 150 cm searchlight Sw. 34 for the heavy AAA units. The latter type, along with its Maschinensatz 33 or 37 generator, was initially mobile when carried on a two-axle Sd.Ah. 102 trailer (later replaced by the twin suspension Sd.Ah. 104).

When weather conditions were good, the illumination range of the 150 cm searchlight was around 10,000 meters horizontally and 12,000 meters at an elevation of 90°. The improved 150 cm Flakscheinwerfer 37 had a range of around 12,000 meters horizontally and 15,000 meters at a 90° elevation. Both types were equipped with an automatic control invert high-intensity lamp, a glass parabolic reflector with a diameter of 150 cm and a 650 m focal length - "invert", meaning that the lamp was suspended upside down in the searchlight housing. The illumination intensity was around 1,100 million candlepower for the 150 cm Sw. 34 and 1,200 million candlepower for the 150 cm Sw. 37.

Power was supplied by the mobile Maschinensatz 33 or 37 with 200 amps, 110 volts and around 24 kW, which was fed to the AAA searchlight via two rubber cables (each 200 meters long, 70 mm2

When the Second World War broke out each searchlight battery was equipped with nine 150 cm Flakscheinwerfer 34 or 37 and a Dunkelsuchgerät 41 darkness search system, plus nine Ringtrichter Richtungshörer (abbreviated RRH) trumpet-type sound locators, which served as locating systems for the searchlights. During the course of the war the number was increased to 16 searchlights per battery.

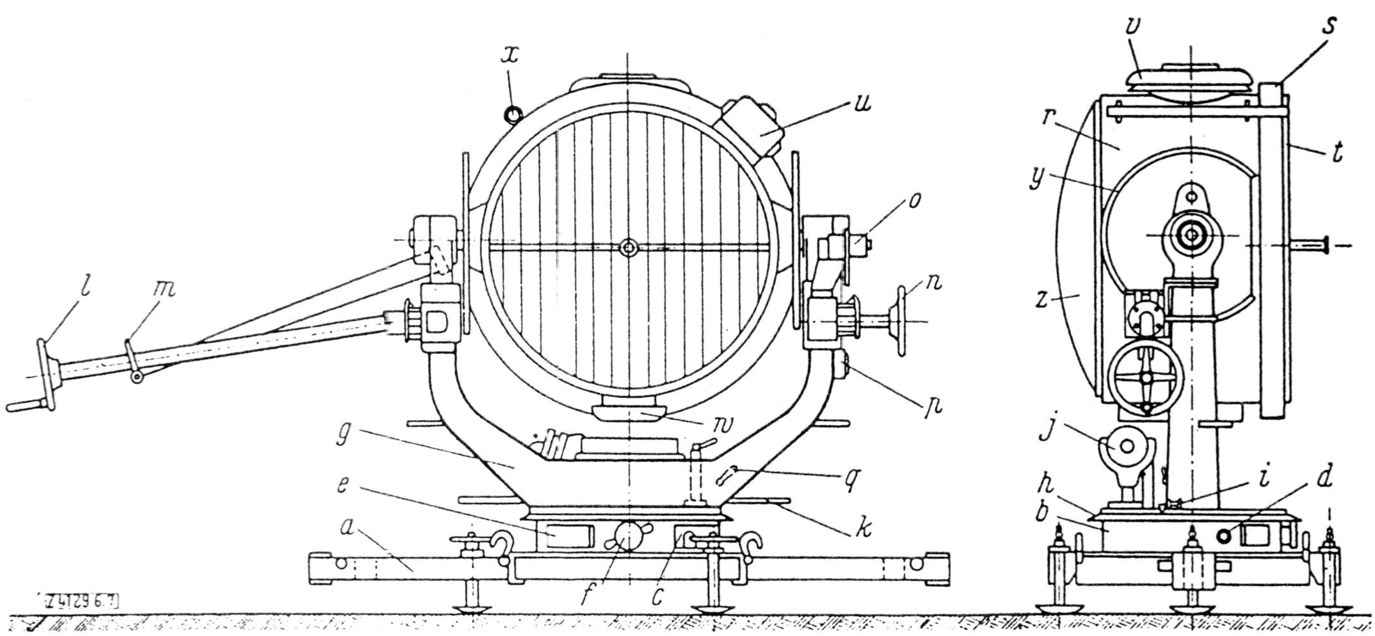

150 cm Searchlight

a) bedplate
b) base
c) connector jacks
d) plug for hand lamp
e) fuzebox
f) plug for data transmitter
g) turntable with support arms
h) graduated circle plate for azimuth
i) illuminated pointer
j) azimuth receiver
k) foot rests
l) guide rod
m) aperture lever
n) elevation handwheel
o) elevation receiver
p) gauge
q) main switch
r) housing
s) aperture
t) cover glass
u) lamp
v) vent
w) chimney valve
x) diopter
y) graduated arc
z) reflector

Right: The 150 cm Flakscheinwerfer 34 on a Sd.Ah. 104 in travel mode, with bedplate lowered.

1) bedplate
2) chassis
12) socket for lock rod
85) guide rod
99) searchlight housing supports
108) lock rod
111) support bearing race
115) opaque ports
157) housing access hatch
112, 158, 159, 161)
162) viewport
163) housing cover
199) guide rod alloy metal shaft with handle
200, 201) connecting flange
202) handwheel
206) leveling stakes
(From L.Dv. 602/2, dia. 4)

Right: 150 cm Sw. 34 with bedplate, reflector side, in operating position. Major parts:
71) elevation receiver with
70) bearing block
85) guide rod with
200) handle
202) handwheel
204) lever for
95) aperture control
201) connecting flange for guide rod and
203) coupling
102) searchlight housing with
114) bell vent above and
115) air inlet louvers below
149) lamp box with
145) hand crank
171) reflector holder
168) diopter and
169) sighting scope
(L.Dv. 602/2, dia. 7)

Right: 150 cm Sw 37, cover glass side, operating position. Main parts:

11) base
22) hand lamp
38) graduated circle plate
50) foot rest
97) cover glass with
167) holder
111) vent
112) air inlet louvers
115) upper viewport
116) lower viewport
124) housing access hatch
129) lamp controller mechanism
168) carbon lead-in tube
178) guide rod
(L.Dv. 601/1, dia. 6)

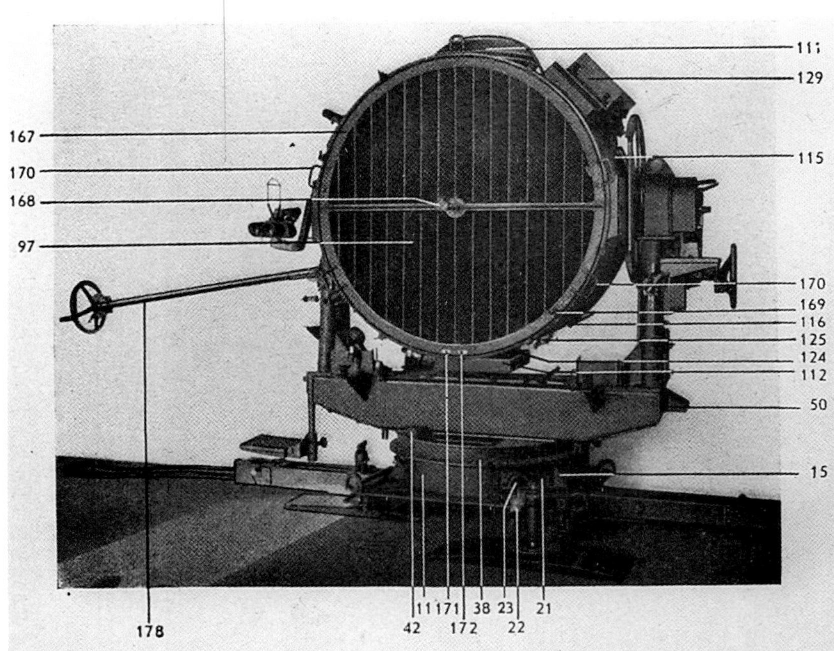

The most obvious difference between the 150 cm Sw. 34 and the 150 cm Sw. 37 can probably be found in the shape of the support arms. On the Sw. 34 these consist of welded iron plate construction, while those on the Sw. 37 are tubular supports, bolted to the turntable. These two photos show the left side of each system. Only the most significant features are identified here. On the left is the 150 cm Sw. 34: (57) main switch, (59) footstep with anti-slip pad, (60,61) fixed foot rests, (65) light, (66) volt/amp meter with (67) light, (69) elevation handwheel, (71) elevation receiver, (73) pointer on elevation arc, (75) bearing block, (76) carbon monitor, (78) hand grip, (185) turnbuckle for cover glass frame, (104) aperture housing, (105) reflector housing, (147) hand crank with raised markings for lamp adjustment, (149) lamp box, (150, 151) access covers, (152) graduated arc, (153) housing lamp switch, (154) pre-illumination switch for pre-illumination lamp, visible through (156) viewport, 165) toothed segment, (171) reflector housing. (L.Dv. 602/2, dia. 13)

Left: 150 cm Sw. 37: (32) elevation receiver, (34) blue glass with button for illuminated signal indicator, (64) left support arm, (81) cover, (82) matte glass and button for pre-illumination, (83) system illumination switch, (86) power and voltage gauge with (87) light, (88) permanent footrest, (89) left graduated arc light, (90) pointer for graduated arc position, (91) upper footrest with hand grip, (92) left vertical movement gearbox, (105) left bearing block, (106) carbon monitor, (115) upper viewport, (118) left toothed segment, (120) left support rail, (122) left spur gear, (155) hand crank for lamp adjustment, (213) sheet metal cover over the limiter for the lamp control device. (L.Dv. 601/1, dia. 11)

Above: 150 cm Sw. 37 searchlights lined up for an inspection on a barracks parade ground.

Below: Training exercise for a searchlight battery on the parade ground of a barracks. The chassis of the two-axle Sd.Ah. 104 trailers have been pulled away and parked in front of and behind the Sw. 37s. Some of the crewmembers are standing behind their searchlights, while others are training on their systems. One of the Ringtrichter-Richtungshörer (RRH) sound locators, also part of the battery complement, has been set up as well. The two listeners and the crewman who operates the acoustic corrector stand behind their system. Other crewmen are being shown the operating functions of the searchlight director. This device aids the air observers in locating a target and for directing the searchlight or RRH to the target. The equipment in the foreground are the power generators for the searchlights.

Left: A 150 cm searchlight in a somewhat modified form. The elevation control operator has a seat on the left. Using headphones he receives elevation data either from a RRH or radar system by voice radio.

Left: This is a rather unusual location for a 150 cm searchlight on the Atlantic seawall. This searchlight was apparently used exclusively against maritime targets. It is permanently mounted on a two-axle trailer which is missing its wheels. Searchlight and trailer rest on folded-up leveling jacks, apparently three on each side. The left side is lacking the elevation graduation arc and the elevation adjusting handwheel.

Left: Among the shifting sand of the dunes, where transport via Sd.Ah. 104 wasn't possible, much effort was required to slide the unloaded 150 cm Sw. 37 into position with the aid of boards and a block and tackle.

Above: Here we see the backside of this 150 cm Sw. 34 searchlight's reflector with the bowl-shaped holder. The guide rod juts out from the right side, and on the left can be seen the elevation graduation arc and the handwheel for vertical adjustment. In the background, behind the searchlight, an RRH sound locator for providing information to the searchlight crew is visible beneath its protective tarp.

Below left: This 150 cm searchlight has, in addition to its labyrinth screen, four moving frames holding four glass sections each and linked by pushrods, mounted in front of the cover glass. For cleaning they're oriented vertically (left), while during operations (below) they were arranged horizontally. In practice these were uncommon.

Above: Searchlights probe the night skies for approaching enemy bombers. The first AAA bursts are already detonating between the beams.

Below: A 150 cm Sw 34 in action. The crew earnestly scan the sky, trying to see if the target has been picked up.

Below: The bushes and cover plate glow brightly under the glare of the cover glass. A directional controller operates the elevation handwheel, while a second checks the carbon feed through the carbon monitor.

Right: Students and apprentices born in the years 1926, 1927 and 1928 were inducted into the Flak during the course of the war as Luftwaffenhelfer (LwH, or Luftwaffe auxiliary forces). This photo shows auxiliary troops being trained by an NCO on a 150 cm searchlight. They're being shown how the guide rod operates. The LwH being instructed probably has a comms link with a sound locator when using the field telephone hanging from the guide rod. In place of a hand receiver he's wearing headphones and has a chest microphone around his neck.

Right: In addition to the Luftwaffe auxiliaries, Flakwaffenhelferinnen (Flakwaffe women's auxiliary forces) were also used on the searchlights and sound locators for the Flak. In this photo the operating crew, consisting of female auxiliaries, have formed up beside their 150 cm Sw. 34.

Right: Female auxiliaries during directional training. The H5 stands at the guide rod. The H2, standing on a supplemental wooden step, looks through the target diopter toward the target. Another crewmember appears to be looking at the graduated circle plate on the base beneath the turntable. The cover for the lighttight slits can be seen on the underside of the housing. Fresh air flowed through these to replace the heated air exiting the housing via the bell vent on the top.

Left: The auxiliary standing behind the H4 at the searchlight aiming device finds the target using the large plotting sight (marked with illuminated paint) and directs the H4. The Scheinwerferrichtungsweiser 35 aiming device was for aiming and directing the searchlights to the target. In order to do so, the devices were set up on a unified base line direction. Magnification of the high powered twin optics was 10x80 and had a field of view of 130 meters at a distance of 1000 meters.

Left: Women's auxiliary troops being trained on the Flakrichtgerät 40A sighting device. This device was fitted with two 10x80 binoculars. Using these, the target could be acquired visually and directional data passed off to the control searchlight.

Left: The H13 and H14 are looking for the target using the binoculars of the sighting device, while the H11 and H12 monitor the directional data being passed by the radar system on the follow-the-pointer gauge of the Übertragungsgerät 37. If the radar wasn't operating the data was passed by voice radio from the sound locator. Once the target was acquired visually they relayed the data to the control searchlight.

Very shortly after the war started it was noticed that the illumination intensity of the 150 cm searchlight was barely adequate for acquiring aerial targets approaching at ever higher altitudes in a timely manner. Accordingly, better performing 200 cm Scheinwerfer 40 A, 40 B and later, the Hochleistungsscheinwerfer 43 were produced, which first became operational in 1943. Up until that time efforts were made to improve the effectiveness of the 150 cm searchlights by mounting four 150 cm searchlights in a combinded quad arrangement on a bridge frame. However, since the idea failed to achieve the hoped-for performance boost, only 61 of these systems went into operation.

The 200 cm AAA searchlight was fitted with an automatic inverted high-performance DC arc lamp, i.e. the carbon was fed in automatically. The required 450 amps at 110 volts was supplied by a Maschinensatz 60 kW generator. This was, as was the 200 cm searchlight, transportable using the two-axle Sonderanhänger 204 trailer. The improved 200 cm Flak-Sw. 43 and its associated 120 kW generator were made mobile by the two-axle Sd.Ah. 206.

A 200 cm searchlight was often used in a 150 cm searchlight platoon as a control searchlight. The more powerful searchlight worked in conjunction with a radar system as a locator, which passed the searchlight directional data to the target via the Übertragungsgerät 37.

Searchlight operations during the night, in hazy or cloudy weather, and even on quite clear nights were of limited effectiveness, if not altogether impossible. It wasn't until the introduction of radar systems that the AAA units were able to achieve success under such weather conditions.

Above: A 200 cm Scheinwerfer 40 in operation.

Below: The 200 cm Flak-Scheinwerfer 40s generally acted as the control searchlights in a searchlight platoon and were linked up with a radar. From the radar the crew received lateral and vertical directional values via the Übertragungsgerät 37 on the follow-the-pointer gauge. Here we see the elevation directional controller seated in front of the elevation receiver, who monitors the receiver's follow-the-pointer with the aid of the elevation control handwheel.

Above: Female auxiliaries cleaning a 200 cm searchlight following night operations. The heavy cover must first be removed from the glass. This was facilitated by two handgrips on either side.

Above: The cover has been removed and now the glass is being cleaned from the outside. One auxiliary keeps her balance by hanging on to the carbon feed tube with one hand.

Below: Here we see the lamp control system which incorporated all the devices needed for controlling the carbon (feed and rotation). Lamp adjustment, moving the positive and negative carbons, as well as the cooling vents were all operated by motors. If these broke down the functions could be switched over to manual control.

Above: Particular care was needed when cleaning the interior of the searchlight. Here one of the Flakwaffe auxiliaries has partially climbed inside the searchlight via the housing access hatch. The reflector, the two rotating mirrors for the carbon monitor and here the glass stripes on the cover glass first had to be cleaned of all carbon ash residue using a brush, then (by regulation) everything had to be wiped down with a damp linen cloth, dried with a wool cloth and finally polished with a chamois.

Above: One auxiliary stands inside the searchlight next to the lamp while another test feeds a carbon stick into the lamps carbon feed tube. The carbon was generally only used during alerts in order to prevent it from going damp. It was stored in a dry state in canisters.

Right: The elevation controller sits in front of his follow-the-pointer receiver while another operator peers through the targt diopter.

Above: Yet another left side view of the 200 cm Sw. 40 searchlight showing the elevation drive and the requisite crewman.

Above: The azimuth controller sits in front of the azimuth receiver. The gauges from the Übertragungsgerät 37 and pointers on both of the dials can be seen clearly in this photograph.

Below: From the reflection, it looks as though the site is upside down when seen in the reflector of the 200 cm Sw. 40.

SOUND LOCATORS, Trumpet-type SOUND LOCATORS (RRH)

Since 1917 the searchlights had worked in conjunction with acoustic locating devices, called dual sound locators (Doppelrichtungshörer, or DRH), for locating targets. Just as a rangefinder amplified the visual range when plotting targets with the eye, the sound locator amplified the audio range. The direction of sound can therefore be determined with much greater accuracy. However, since sound travels 333 meters per second under normal atmospheric conditions there is a considerable time lag between the originator - the aircraft - and the ears of the listener. During this interval the target, depending on distance and speed, can cover much ground. Using an acoustic corrector with the sound locator, the target's course between its present and future positions can be determined based on its movement and estimated speed. These new directional data, corrected for course changes, were passed to the searchlights either telephonically or electrically via signal light indicators. However, this method did not take into account atmospheric conditions such as wind, clouds and temperatures, all of which affected sound, so that it was hoped the searchlight, using the directional values from the sound locator, would be able to acquire the target when it first turned on its beam; longer unsuccessful searching would give away the searchlight's position.

The most common dual sound locator design consisted of two base frames mounted perpendicular to each other, each having two cones; a listener would use one cone pair to determine the azimuth, while the second operator determined the altitude with the second pair.

Most of the sound locators employed by the Wehrmacht during the Second World War were of the type using four funnels mounted to a ring, hence the name "Ringtrichter-Richtungshörer", abbreviated RRH (literally translated as "funnel ring sound locator", but generally known as a trumpet-type sound locator). Unlike with other types, it was no longer necessary to remove the listening cones when transporting the system, nor was it necessary to have the device precisely leveled when moving from one site to another. Sound location accuracy was around °2° with the RRH. However, the sound values from around 5 km to 12 km were highly dependent on the current weather conditions, surrounding disturbances, the engine noise generated by the aircraft to be located and the listening capabilities of the operators. When the listeners, after adjusting the locator laterally and vertically, were to get the impression that the sound waves generated by the aircraft targeted are being received at precisely the same moment in both ears - felt as a sensation in the center part of the back of the head - they call out "Mitteleindruck!" (lit. center feeling), meaning the target has been acquired.

With the increasing flying altitudes and speeds sound location results soon became less and less satisfactory and radar systems took over the role of providing data for the searchlights. However, since the number of radars was insufficient (due to their primary role of supporting flak batteries) and they were sometimes jammed by the enemy, the sound locators proved indispensable.

During the first year of the war, the RRH served as directional locators for flak batteries in foggy or cloudy conditions when searchlights couldn't operate effectively. But since target altitude and distance can't be measured by an RRH, trials were carried out using two sound locator plots. However, there was too much lag time between the RRH and the fire control system, so that without a radar system only controlled barrage fire could be thrown up.

Despite these shortcomings there were still 5,559 trumpet-type sound locators in action as late as August of 1944.

The RRH comprised a 732 kg baseplate, base holder, column, two support arms, the funnel ring, lateral and vertical drives and the acoustic corrector. The system was portable on a two-axle Sd.Ah. 104 trailer. The listening squad consisted of a commander, the K10; the K7 sat at the acoustic corrector at the back of the locator; on the left, the K8 sat at the azimuth handwheel and acted as a listener for azimuth; the K9 sat at the right on the elevation handwheel and listened for altitude. Both listeners had to have particularly good hearing capabilities, which were sharpened through regularly conducted listening exercises.

Below: A dual sound locator with searchlight during WWI. The horizontal (1) and vertical (2) sound cones were linked to the searchlight. Tubes of equal length (3,4) led from the cones to the listeners. Step plate (5) and headrest (6) for the vertical listener, target scope (7) and counterbalance (8) are other features of this system.

Left: A somewhat older listening system with separate cones, although this was also used during the Second World War. On the right and left are the horizontal cones for determining the azimuth to the target, while above and below are the vertical cones for determining the elevation angle. The Sw. 37 located at the edge of the forest is linked to the sound locator; its guide rod has been removed and rests next to the searchlight. The directional controller adjusts the searchlight based on the data passed by radiotelephone from the sound locator.

Left: Night operation of a sound locator. The tubes running from the cones to the listeners are clearly visible in this photo.

Left: This listening device is in the Wehrtechnisches Museum in Coblenz. Using this system, targets could be acquired out to a range of 12,000 meters (depending on weather conditions). Target acquisition accuracy was 2°. It required a three-man crew - an azimuth director, an elevation director and an operator for the acoustic corrector (seen on the right in picture). From here the target data was passed to the flak searchlights, with compensation for target movement and the distance which the target covered from the time it gave off a sound until the same was picked up by the listeners. The calculations were carried out within the acoustic corrector mechanically.

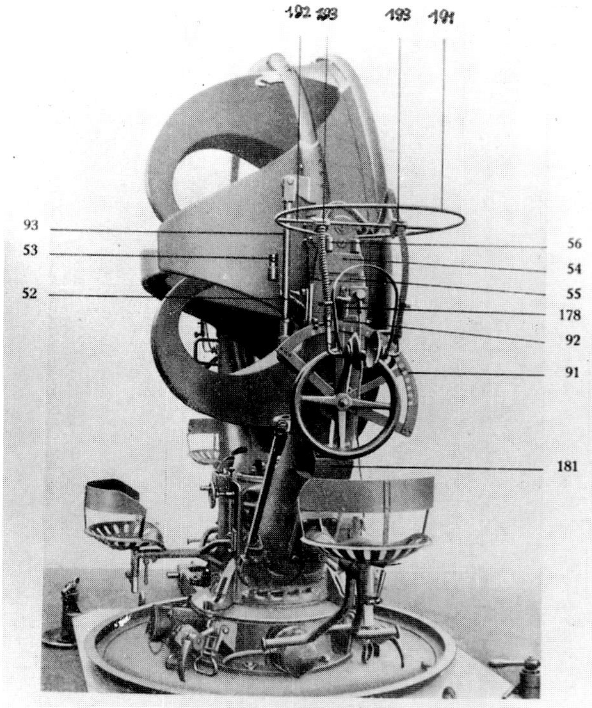

The listening device most commonly used in the Second World War was the trumpet-type sound locator (RRH). This system had the four sound funnels attached to a ring, obviating the need for precise leveling of the individual funnels when the system was moved. Above, we see the right side of the RRH with stop gauge (52), rubber buffers (53), bearing block (54), rubber gap bearing (55), lugs (56), acoustic graduation arc (91), acoustic elevation pointer (92), pushrod (93), lights for acoustic elevation pointer (178), elevation signal transmitter (181), rain cover support ring with crossbrace and clamps (191). (L.DV. 604, dia. 9)

Above right: Front side of the system with manufacturer's plate (13), cap (41), seat support shaft (45), seat shaft crossbar (46), ball grip (48), seat (49), foot rest (50), hand grip (51), elevation handwheel (77), azimuth handwheel (78), azimuth gauge (148). (L.Dv. 604, dia. 1)

Right: The listeners on this RRH sit beneath their individual tents, which have been drawn around the seats on curtain rings designed for the tents. The searchlight linked to the sound locator can just be seen to the left in the picture.

Above: Trumpet-type sound locators, together with their searchlights in the background, have been drawn up in a line on their Sonderanhänger 104 trailers at a barracks parade ground.

Left: An RRH in operating position. The two chassis of the Sd.Ah. 104 have been moved a few meters away from the device. The forward chassis has the coupling shaft, while above that is the handbrake and to the right the handcrank for raising and lowering the device, and the air cylinder for the airbrakes crossways between the two fenders.

Left: Here we see the RRH's three crewmen at their stations. On the left the K8 operates the azimuth funnels, the K9 sits on the right for the elevation funnels and the K7 in the center operates the acoustic corrector. On the RRH the acoustic corrector was permanently linked to the sound locator. The white collar tabs on the crewmen reveal that they belong to the "General Göring" regiment.

Right: Luftwaffe auxiliaries were also trained and used on RRH systems. Here an NCO explains the function of the acoustic corrector to these youth.

Below: Luftwaffe auxiliary troops have formed up for instruction next to their RRH. The opinion of many supposedly more competent persons regarding the "Baby-Flak" (as they were sometimes derisively called) quickly changed, for the youth performed amazingly well in action and were often more committed to their work than many older soldiers.

Below: Here a prime mover is seen towing a covered RRH to its operating site through rough terrain. The tactical markings on the fenders of the RRH trailer and on the rear of the prime mover reveal that this searchlight battery was part of the "General Göring" regiment.

Left: Alert for the Flakwaffe auxiliaries, scrambling to an RRH. They're carrying steel helmets, gas masks and ponchos needed when operating the device. The listeners also have their seat cushions with them. A rain cover still hides the sound locator.

Below: The H7 sits with gas mask, gas poncho and steel helmet. The listeners kept these things close at hand, since they were hindrances when worn during sound locating operations.

Below: The H8 listens attentively at the azimuth controller, waiting to see when the aircraft sounds echo simultaneously in both her ears and she then has the requisite "center feeling" in her head. When both listeners announced a "center feeling", the device was correctly honed in on the target and the predictor data could be passed on to the searchlights after being determined by the acoustic corrector.